T0131266

AN ABC OF INDIAN FOOD

TO MY FRIEND
MERCEDES WEBB
WHO SHARES MY
LOVE OF INDIA

AN A B C OF INDIAN FOOD

JOYCE P. WESTRIP

WITH ILLUSTRATIONS BY
MERCEDES WEBB AND PHILIPPA STOCKLEY

PROSPECT BOOKS
1996

First published in Great Britain, 1996

by

Prospect Books,

Allaleigh House, Blackawton, Totnes, Devon TQ9 7DL.

A CIP record for this book is available from the British Library.

ISBN 0907325718

Printed by The Cromwell Press, Broughton Gifford, Wiltshire.

CONTENTS

Acknowledgements

I hasten to thank the authors whose books are listed in the
bibliography to which I reached out on many occasions to check
and re-check my research; and Shakuntala Devagnanam who had
the answers to several queries. My collection of menus from Indian
restaurants round the world were an invaluable source of
information. I give special thanks to Pat Chapman for kindling and
keeping alight culinary interest in India through *The Curry Club
Magazine*. I thank also Mercedes Webb for her cheerful assistance
at all times and for providing illustrations; and my husband Charles
for his patience.

INTRODUCTION

The evolution of the cooking style of India reaches back into antiquity. The vast sub-continent with over 900 million people, now with 15 principal languages and 1,650 dialects has, over thousands of years, experienced invasions by the Aryans, the Huns, the Scythians, the Arabs, the Persians, the Greeks, the Turks, the Pathans, the Moghuls, the Portuguese, the Dutch, the French and the British. Layer upon layer of new cultural strains have been absorbed by conqueror and conquered alike to make India the diverse country it is today. Food patterns reflect these same political and cultural upheavals and it is their variety that makes eating in India a very special affair for the traveller.

Unfamiliarity with names of ingredients, different methods of cooking, and names of dishes have, in the past, prevented many people from enjoying what should be one of the highlights of their journey: the food.

No experience of India would be complete without tasting as many of the regional styles of cooking as possible: from the rojan goshts (or josh or gosh) of Kashmir, to Delhi's Moghlai badami murgh, or the fish and seafood specialities of Bengal such as macher jhol cooked in mustard oil, and the very typical sweets, rasgullas and sandesh, that come from there also. Indians enjoy their sweets and puddings made from fruits, cereals, nuts and vegetables or from milk and cream; one pudding-type dish is called kheer or khir in North India, payasam in South India, payash in East India. In Bombay, Parsi-style dishes such as dhansak and akoorie should not be missed nor must the robust vindaloos, xacuttis and sorpotels of Goa; and a feast of utter delight would be to run the gastronomic gamut of the styles of kababs such as shammi, pasinda, reshmi, sheekh and kakori kababs. Travel to South India, where vegetarianism comes into its own, to sample the thali meals of Madras, the aviyals and pongals of Kerala and the renowned idlis of Udipi prepared by cooks temple-trained to cook first for the gods.

The markets are a photographer's dream with mountains of vegetables such as palak, gajar, bhindi or lady's fingers, purple-black baigan or eggplant, enormous chillies—green and red—glistening in the sunlight, and fresh green coriander in huge baskets sitting alongside piles of garlic and ginger. India abounds too in exotic fruits—jackfruit, pomegranates, custard apples—and when it is the season for mangoes, there is no better way to end a meal. Luscious mangoes named Alphonso, Jahangir, Langra and Gulabkash are just a few of the varieties.

If you show an interest and curiosity about the food, you will be made welcome and win friends. Indians are very hospitable people, and they are proud of the styles of cuisine that have evolved over 5,000 years. It is part of their culture to offer food to a stranger—after all you may be a God in disguise.

How to use this book

This pocket companion is intended for the reader interested in the food of India. It can be used in several ways.

You will find it a useful ready-reference in restaurants as you ponder over the menus. Use it as a guide to identify ingredients in the market place. Try out new recipes with confidence now that unfamiliar names and culinary terms are here explained.

It will introduce you to a range of spices, which is the common fusing factor of cooking in India, and to myriad other ingredients. It gives the names and a brief description of many recipes that you will encounter as you venture on your gastronomic quest.

It will help you identify the main ingredients in a dish and you will soon gain more confidence in selecting what you want to order in a restaurant. A dish on the menu contains the word 'murgh': turn to the right page and discover that 'murgh' is chicken.

The index provides a cross-reference, useful particularly for travellers. If, in a restaurant, chicken is your fancy, you will find all entries in the *ABC* that have connections with the bird listed in the index. Look up the relevant page and place your order.

Hindi is the *lingua franca* of India and much of the *ABC* consists of Hindi names. However, there are dishes and ingredients that relate to a certain region: for instance, a sweet breakfast dish from south India made from pounded rice and coconut called puttu or pootu. This is the Tamil name, and I have listed it in that language. In the index, the entry is under rice, the main ingredient.

You will often find variations in the spelling of transliterated words in India. Cheera, chura, or chewra are three interpretations of one mix of spiced nibbles. I have not gone to the extreme length of giving every alternative a main entry to itself, rather I have classified each item under the version most often encountered, giving variations a subordinate place. To cope with the spelling problem, one simply has to tune into the phonetics. The transliterations in this book have no diacritical marks or accents: this is commonly accepted in modern Indian publishing.

When you return home and begin cooking Indian-style, I hope this *ABC* will have given you the courage you needed to eat anything and everything on your travels. In turn, it should help your experiments in your own kitchen: no more feeling daunted that a recipe may contain an unfamiliar ingredient.

I sometimes think that various usages of the English language need their own glossary, so I have made the English part of the text comprehensible to American and Australian as well as British readers by giving the standard variants such as eggplant for aubergine, cream of wheat for semolina and so on.

A

AAB GOSHT	Spiced lamb stew
AAM/AHM	Mango, the fruit of the tree *Mangifera indica*
AAM CHUR	Mango powder, used as a flavouring agent
ACHAR	Pickle
ADDAKA	Areca, the nut of the palm tree *Areca catechu* (South India)
ADRAK	Ginger, the rhizome of the plant *Zingiber officinale*

AJWAIN	Ajowan seeds, also known as bishop's weed, *Carum ajowan;* used to flavour fried snacks and lentils and root vegetables
AKHNI	Light vegetable stock
AKHROOT	Walnut, the nut of the tree *Juglans regia*
AKNOR JHOL	Spiced broth (Bengal)
AKOORI	Scrambled eggs with fresh chilli and coriander, Parsi style
ALEBELE	Sweet pancake, tea-time snack (Goa)
ALOO/ALU	Potato
ALOO BOKHARA	Dried plum, the fruit of the tree *Prunus domestica*, used as a flavouring to add tartness
ALOO CHAT	Tamarind-flavoured potato snack
ALOO CHIDWA	Deep-fried savoury potato snack
ALOO CHOP	An Anglo-Indian dish of savoury mince encased in mashed potato; or balls of spiced, mashed potato, batter-dipped and deep-fried
ALOO DUM	Potatoes spiced and steamed

ALOO GOBI	Potatoes with cauliflower
ALOO MATTAR	Potatoes with peas
ALOO METHI	Potatoes and fenugreek
ALOO PALAK	Potatoes and spinach
ALOO TIKKIS	Spiced potato patties
AMJOOD	Parsley
AMLA	Green gooseberries, fruit of the plant *Ribes uvacrispa*
AMRITI	Flour-based halwa sweet
AMROOD	Guava, the fruit of the tree of the myrtle family, *Psidium guajava*
AMTI	Spiced lentil dish with sweet and sour flavourings of jaggery and tamarind
ANANAS	Fresh pineapple
ANAR	Fresh pomegranate, the fruit of the tree *Punica granatum*
ANARDANA	Dried pomegranate seeds, used as flavouring
ANDA	Egg
ANDWARI	Fish of the mullet family, *Mugildae*

ANGOOR	Fresh grapes
ANJEER	Figs
APPAMS/HOPPERS	Crisp-collared pancakes of rice flour and coconut milk (South India)
APUPA	Cakes made from rice or barley flour, deep-fried and immersed in a syrup of honey
ARAK/ARACK	Intoxicating drink from the coconut palm *Cocos nucifera*
ARBI/ARVI KI PATTA	Leaves of the taro plant (*Colocasia antiquorum*) spread with a spiced paste of gram flour, stacked, rolled, steamed and fried; popular in Bombay
ARECA	The nut from the palm *Areca catechu* eaten with betel leaf for its astringency
ARHAR DAL	Hulled and split yellow pulse, also known as toor or toovar dal
ARHOO	Fresh peach
ARISI	Rice (South India)
AROOQ	Deep-fried pungent patties of minced lamb, chicken or fish

ARWA CHAVAL/CHAWAL	Long-grain rice
ASSAD	Meat and potatoes in a spiced sauce (Goa)
ATHIRASA/ATHIRASAM	Deep-fried cakes sweetened with jaggery (South India)
ATTA	Wholemeal or wholewheat flour
AVIL UPPUMA	Savoury made from flattened rice (South India)
AVIYAL	Vegetables cooked in coconut milk and yoghurt (South India)

B

BAASI	Stale
BADA	Savoury snack of deep-fried lentil balls
BADAIN	Star anise, fruit of the *Illicium verum*
BADAM/BADAMI	Almond
BAFFAD	Dry curry of pork and radish (Goa)
BAIGAN/BAINGAN	Egg plant or aubergine, fruit of the *Solanum melongena*
BAJJI/BHAJIA	Vegetables batter-dipped and deep-fried, and served as a snack

BAJRI	Millet, edible grain, *Eleusine coracana*
BAKALA BATH	Yoghurt rice
BAKARKHANI	Leavened layered cardamom-flavoured griddle-fried bread
BAKLA	Broad beans
BAKRA/BAKRI KA GOSHT	Lamb
BAKRI KA DOODH	Goat's milk
BALAM	Long-grain rice from Bangladesh
BALCHAO	Dried prawn and chilli relish
BALUSHAHI	Deep-fried syrup-coated pastry
BHANDGOBI	Cabbage
BARA/BOORA	Ball of lentils, vegetables or fish, deep-fried and immersed in sauce
BARAF	Ice
BARFI/BURFI	Fudge-type milk sweet
BASMATI	Aromatic long-grain rice
BATAKH	Duck
BATAIR	Quail
BATATA	Potato

BATURAS/BHATURAS	Deep-fried sweet dough discs
BEBINCA	Layered cake (Goa)
BEKTI/BHEKTI	Fish of the perch family, *Lates cacarifer* (Bengal)
BESAN	Chick pea flour
BEVECA	Rice pudding flavoured with coconut (Goa)
BHAGAR	Whole spices or seasonings tempered in hot ghee or oil, added to cooked dishes
BHAGHARE BAINGAN/BAIGAN	Miniature aubergines or eggplant, flavoured with tamarind, coconut, sesame and poppy seeds (Hyderabad)
BHAINS KA DOODH	Buffalo milk
BHAPA DHAI	Saffron-flavoured, steamed dessert (Bengal)
BHARTA/BHURTA	Spiced mashed vegetables, oven-baked
BHAT/BHATH	Plain boiled rice
BHEJA	Brain
BHEL POORIE	A spiced mixture of puffed rice, vermicelli, poorie pieces and

	potato, flavoured with tamarind juice—popular street food in the Bombay region
BHEN	Lotus root, the rhizome of *Nelumbium nuciferum*
BHINDI	Okra, gumbo or lady's fingers
BHONA/BHOONA	Process of frying masalas
BHOPLA	Ash gourd, *Benincasa hispida* (Bengal)
BHUKI/BHUJEE	Lightly spiced stir-fried mixed vegetables
BHUNA GOSHT	Dry-fried spiced meat
BIRAHI/BIRHIO	An unleavened bread of wheat flour with a chick pea dough filling
BIRYANI	Oven-baked, parboiled rice layered with nuts, fruit, meat and spices
BOLO PADRE	Coconut and semolina or cream of wheat-flour cake (Goa)
BOMBAY DUCK	Dried pungent, salted fish, *Harpodon nephereus*, broiled or fried and served as an accompaniment; also known as salt fish and bommaloe maachi

BONDA	Spiced potato balls, batter-dipped and deep-fried, served as a snack
BOONDI	Tiny crisp, deep-fried batter balls steeped in syrup
BOORANI	Yoghurt-onion (raita) side dish
BOTI KABAB	Cubes of lamb marinated and cooked in a tandoor oven
BRINJAL	Aubergine or eggplant, fruit of the plant *Solanum melongena*

C

CACHUMBER/KACHAMBER	Chopped onion, tomato, chilli served as an accompaniment
CAFREAL	Chicken pieces hot with chillies (Goa)
CAJOU	Cashew nut
CALDINE	Fish, eggs or vegetables in a yellow-coloured liquid sauce (Goa)
CALDO VERDE	Spinach soup (Goa)
CHA/CHAI	Tea
CHAAT	Teatime fruit or vegetable snack

CHAKLI	Deep-fried spirals of batter made from chick pea flour
CHAKNA	Spiced offal (Hyderabad)
CHANDA	The white or silver pomfret fish, *Pampus argenteus* (Bengal)
CHANDAN	Sandalwood, from the tree *Santalum album*
CHANNA	Hulled and split yellow pulse of the chick pea family, *Cicer arietinum*
CHANNA BATURA	Deep-fried discs of chick pea flour
CHAPATI/CHAPPATI	Unleavened bread dry-cooked on a hot griddle
CHARCHARI	Smoked vegetables
CHANTANI/CHATNI	Chutney; sweet or pungent relish
CHAWAL	Rice
CHEENEE/CHINI	Sugar (South India)
CHEERA/CHURA/CHEWRA	Mixed savoury nibbles
CHENNA/CHHANA	Cheesy curd dough used in many sweet dishes
CHENNEL	Variety of rice, red in colour
CHETTINAD	An area in Tamil Nadu, home to this style of cooking

CHHAS	Buttermilk (Gujarat)
CHHUNDO	Sweet cardamom-flavoured mango chutney
CHICHINGA/CHAHEHIND	Snake gourd, *Tricosanthes anguina* (Bengal)
CHIDWA	Spiced nibbles
CHIKKI	Sweet made from wheat flour with sesame seeds or nuts
CHILGOSE	Small cream-coloured pine nuts, *Pinus geradiana*
CHINGRI	Shrimps, prawns (Bengal)
CHOLE/CHHOLE	Spiced chick pea dish
CHORMAGAZ	Melon seeds
CHOTEE GOBI/CHAUNK GOBI	Brussel Sprouts
CHOURISO/CHOURICO	Spiced sausage (Goa)
CHOWLA	Black-eyed beans (UK), cowpeas (US), *Vigna unguiculata*
CHUKARAI	Sugar
CHUKANDER	Beetroot or beet
CHUNAM	Edible lime taken with paan (betel)
CURAMBA	Mango cooked with semolina

D

DAHI BARA/DAHI VADA	Lentil dough balls in yoghurt sauce
DAHI MACHHI	Fish cooked in a spiced yoghurt sauce
DAHI/DOI	Plain yoghurt
DAL/DHAL	Generic term for the lentil or pulse family when split
DALCHA	Tamarind-flavoured lamb and lentil dish
DALCHINI	Cinnamon, dried bark of the tree *Cinnamomum zeylanicum*

DALIA	Cracked wheat
DALMA	Lentils with vegetables including green banana
DEGI MIRCH	Chilli powder
DHAN	Unhusked rice
DHANESAG	Coriander leaves
DHANIA	Coriander, *Coriandrum sativum*
DHANSAK	Meat or chicken in a spiced purée of four or more sorts of lentils (Parsi)
DHOKLA/DHOKRI	Savoury, steamed gram-flour cake (Gujarat)
DHUNAUR	Mixed spices
DILBHAR	Milk sweet made with a soft cheese dough (Bengal)
DOL DOL	Coconut flavoured, halwa-like sweet made from dark glutinous rice flour (South India)
DOODH	Milk
DOODH PAK	Fragrant rice pudding
DOODH PEDA	Milk fudge often garnished with nuts

DOPIAZA/DOPYAZ	Meat dish with an abundance of onions (Hyderabad)
DOSA/DOSAI/THOSAI	Fermented rice-flour pancake
DUBBLE KA MEETHA	Fragrant bread pudding (Hyderabad)
DUM/DHUM	Method of steaming
DUM ALOO/ALU	Spiced stuffed potatoes
DUM PHUKT	Method of steaming (particularly biryanis) in a vessel sealed with dough (Lucknow)

E

EERAZ	Liver
ELAICHI	Cardamom seed; from the plant *Elettaria cardamomum*
EMPADINHAS	Crusty pies filled with minced or ground prawns or pork (Goa)

F

FALOODA	Sweet milk drink
FARFAS	Cumin-flavoured crisp nibbles
FENI	Intoxicating drink made from coconut or cashew nut (Goa)
FIRNI	Almond-flavoured creamy rice-flour dessert
FOFOS	Fish croquettes (Goa)
FOOGATH	Lightly spiced blanched vegetable dish

G

GAI KA DOODH	Cow's milk
GAI KA GOSHT	Beef
GAIHUN	Wheat
GAJA	Flaky savoury nibbles
GAJAR	Carrot
GAJAR HALWA	Carrot sweetmeat
GANNA	Sugarcane, *Saccharum officinale*
GARAM	Hot
GARAM MASALA	Blend of ground spices
GHEE	Clarified butter

GHIYA	Bottle gourd, *Lagenaria siceraria*
GINGELLY	Sesame oil
GIRDA	Bouncy or chewy-textured leavened wheat bread (Kashmir)
GOCHIAN	Black beehive-shaped mushroom, *Marchella esculenta* (Kashmir)
GOJJU	Mixed vegetables (South India)
GOLGOPPAS	Tiny dough discs, deep-fried to puff up, then served with spiced juice.
GOSHT	Meat
GOSHTABA	Velvety smooth meatballs in a light cardamom-flavoured sauce (Kashmir)
GUL RUH	Rose essence or extract
GULAB JAL	Rose water
GULAB JAMUN	Deep-fried milk-powder dough balls steeped in rose-scented syrup
GUR	Palm sugar—also known as jaggery
GURDE	Kidneys

H

HALDI	Turmeric, from the rhizome of the *Curcuma longa*
HALDI PEESI	Turmeric powder
HALEEM	Meat and spices cooked with cracked wheat
HALWA	Soft sweetmeat made with cereals, vegetables, lentils or fruit and nuts
HANDWA	Savoury cake of coarsely ground rice and chick pea flour (Gujarat)
HARE DHANIA	Fresh coriander
HARE GOBI	Broccoli

HARE MATAR	Green peas
HARE MIRCH	Green capsicum, bell pepper or chilli
HARISO	Custard dessert flavoured with cardamom and nutmeg
HARISSA/HAREES	Ground meat and wheat dish
HATTICHAK	Artichoke
HILSA	A fish (*Clupeia ilisha*) resembling shad
HING	Asafoetida: powdered resin from the root of the plant *Ferula asafoetida*
HIRAN KA GOSHT	Venison
HUSAINI	Lamb on skewers cooked in a mild curry sauce (North India)

I

IDDYAPPAM	Steamed, thin spiralled layers of rice-flour dough (South India)
IDLI/IDDLI	Breakfast steamed rice-flour cakes, with coconut chutney and spiced sauce or sambhar (South India)
IMLI	Tamarind, the fleshy fruit pod from the tree *Tamarindus indica*
INGI	Fresh ginger (South India)
ISABGOL	Psyllium (*Psyllium indica*, the Indian variety of the herb fleawort)—used as a laxative, in powdered form

J

JAGGERY	Raw sugar extracted from the palmyra palm, sugar cane or date palm
JAIPHAL	Nutmeg, the seed of the tree *Myristica fragrans*
JALEBI/JELABI	Spirals of batter, deep-fried and steeped in syrup
JALFREIZI	Stir-fried dishes
JAMIKAND/ZAMIKAND	Yam, the tuber of the genus *Dioscorea*
JAVATRI/JAVITRI	Mace

JAWAR	Barley
JEEB	Tongue
JEERA	Cumin: the seed of *Cuminum cyminum*
JHINGA	Prawns
JHOL	Spiced soup

K

KABAB/KEBAB	Skewered flesh, fish, or vegetables generally cooked over coals
KABLI CHANA	Dried chick peas
KABUTAR	Pigeon
KACHA	Raw
KACHA AAM	Green mango
KACHA KELA	Green plaintain
KACHORI	Deep-fried pastries with a savoury filling
KADALI CHAMPA	Ripe banana (South India)
KADDU	Vegetable marrow, *Cucurbita pepo*

KAHVA/KHAWA	Green tea, flavoured with cardamom and almonds (Kashmir)
KAITH	Woodapple, the fruit of the tree *Feronia limonia*
KAJU	Cashew nut
KAKARI	Cucumber (South India)
KALA JAMUNS	Dark-coloured, deep-fried balls of cheese-curd dough
KALAKAI	Peanuts or groundnuts, *Archis hypogaea* (South India)
KALAN	Green plantain in yoghurt
KALI MIRCH	Black pepper or peppercorn
KALIA	Spiced lamb stew (Hyderabad)
KALIJA/KALEJI	Liver
KALONJI	Nigella seed
KAMARAKH	Star fruit, of two varieties: one is used as a souring agent, from the tree *Averrhoa bilimbi*; the other sweeter, the *Averrhoa carambola*, and is made into chutney
KAMARGAH	Ribbed lamb chops coated with spiced batter (Kashmir)

KANJI	Water in which rice has been cooked
KARADI	Safflower: seeds from the plant *Carthamus tinctorius*
KARANANJIA	Sweet pastry with coconut filling
KARELA	Bitter gourd, *Momordica charantia*
KARHI	Lightly spiced yoghurt and lentil sauce
KARHI PATTA	Leaves from the tree *Murraya koenigii* used as a flavouring, known as curry leaves
KARI	Spiced sauce
KARIVEPPILAI	As karhi patta above, curry leaves (South India)
KARPOOR	Edible camphor
KASHI	Whole chicken stuffed and marinated
KASOORI	Savoury nibbles, fenugreek-flavoured dough crisps
KATHAL	Soft, fleshy, pungent fruit of the tree *Artocarpus integrifolia*, of the same genus as breadfruit

KEEMA/KHIMA	Spiced minced or ground meat
KELA	Banana or plantain used in cooking
KENKRA	Crab
KERI	Green mango
KESAR	Saffron
KESARI/KESARI BATH	Sweet semolina or vermicelli pudding
KEWRA RUH	Screwpine essence extracted from the leaves of the plant *Pandanus odoratissimus*, used for fragrance and flavour
KHAGINA	Ginger-flavoured scrambled egg (Hyderabad)
KHAJUR	Dates from the palm *Phoenix dactylifera*
KHAMIR	Wheat
KHANDOI	Lentil balls in spiced sauce
KHANDVI	Lentil-flour dough rolls garnished with mustard and sesame seeds
KHARBOOJA	Musk melon, the scented netted melon *Cucumis melo*
KHASI KA GOSHT	Goat meat

KHATTE	Sour
KHEER/KHIR	Milk pudding thickened with rice flour
KHEERA/KHIRA	Cucumber
KHICHDI/KHICHRI	Rice cooked with lentils
KHOA/KHOYA	Fresh milk condensed; milk solids used for sweets
KHOOBANI/KHUMANI	Apricot, the fruit of *Prunus armeniaca*
KHUS KHUS/KUS KUS	White poppy seeds, *Papaver somniferum*
KICHLI	Orange (South India)
KID GOSHT	Lamb braised in coconut milk with cashew nuts
KIRIMA	Lentil dish with peas
KISH MISH	Raisins
KOFTAS	Balls of minced meat or vegetables
KOKUM	Sour, deep-red plum from the tree *Garcinia indica*, used as a souring agent (South India)
KOORAL	Vegetables cooked in a moist sauce (South India)

KOOTUS	Lightly-spiced vegetables (South India)
KORMA	A north Indian dish of spiced braised meat or vegetables in a rich sauce
KOTHAMALLI	Coriander leaves (South India)
KOVIPPU	Cauliflower (South India)
KOZHI	Chicken (South India)
KUL KULS	Sugar-syrup-coated pastry scrolls (South India)
KULCHA	Leavened bread discs
KULFI	A firm-textured ice cream made with reduced or condensed milk
KULIA	Milk fudge cake
KUT	Purée usually made from tomatoes flavoured with tamarind

L

LADDU/LADDOOS	A sweetmeat of cardamom flavoured balls of gram flour or semolina dough with nuts
LAL MIRCH	Red capsicum or bell pepper
LAPHRA	Mixed vegetable soup (Bengal)
LASUN/LEHSAN	Garlic
LASSI	A refreshing drink of yoghurt and crushed ice, served sweetened 'lassi methi', or salt 'lassi namkeen'
LATCHE	Deep-fried potato straws
LAUNG	Cloves

LAZEEZ	Chicken kebabs made with a green masala paste
LAZIZAN	Khichdi-style rice dish (Gujarat)
LEECHI/LYCHEE	Juicy white fleshy fruit from the tree *Litchi chinensis*
LENTILS	Dried pulse of many varieties, *Lens esculenta*
LOBHIA	Black-eyed beans in Britain, cowpea in the US, *Vigna unguiculata*
LOOCHI/LUCHI	Bread which puffs upon deep-frying (Bengal)
LOOKME/LUKMI	Deep-fried pastry patties with spiced mince filling
LOUKI	Bottle gourd, *Lagenaria siceraria*

M

MAACHI/MACHHI/MACHI	General name for fish in most regions
MACCHAR JHOL	Lightly spiced fish stew (Bengal)
MADHUR	Honey
MAHAN BHOG	Halwa-type sweet (Bengal)
MAHAPRASAD	Food offering to the Gods
MAHARAJI	Apple (Kashmir)
MAHSEER	The freshwater fish *Barbus tor*, resembling the barbel
MAIDA	White flour

MAKHAN/MUKHAN	Butter
MAKKA/MAKKI	Corn or maize
MALAI	Cream made from layers of skin skimmed from simmering milk
MALPOORA	Pancake served with rose-flavoured syrup
MAMPAZHAM/MAMBALAM	Ripe mango, the fruit of the tree *Mangifera indica* (South India)
MANJAL	Turmeric, from the rhizome of the plant *Curcuma longa* (South India)
MANJAL MULLANGI	Carrot (South India)
MARAG	Aromatic meat broth
MASALA	Mixed spices
MASALA DOSAI	Rice-flour pancakes with spiced potato filling
MASSOR/MASUR DAL	Hulled and split tiny salmon-coloured pulse (*Lens esculenta*), which on cooking turns yellow
MATHRI	Tangy deep-fried crisp savouries
MATTAR	Green peas
MATTU ERAICHI	Beef (South India)

MEEN	A general term for fish (South India)
METHI	Fenugreek: the leaves and seeds of the plant *Trigonella foenum-graecum*, used for flavouring
MILAGAI	Chilli (South India)
MILAGU	Black pepper (South India)
MIRICH HARA	Green chilli
MIRICH LAL	Red chilli
MITHAI/MEETHA	General name for sweets
MODAK	Rice-flour dumplings
MOGHLAI	Style of cooking from Moghul times
MOLEE	Spiced coconut flavoured sauce, a base for chicken, fish or vegetables
MOOLAY	Brain
MOOLE	Large white radish, *Raphanus sativus*
MOONG/MUNG DAL	Hulled and split yellow pulse (*Phaseolus aureus*); when unhulled and whole, the small green and cylindrical shape is known as sabat moong

MOONFALLI	Roasted peanuts
MOORI/MURMURA	Puffed rice
MORRUL	Fish of the sole family, *Ophiocephalus striatus cynoglossus*
MOSAMBI	Sweet lime; orange
MOTAI	Egg (South India)
MULLIGATAWNY	Spiced soup from lamb or chicken stock (Anglo-Indian)
MUNACCA	Raisins and sultanas
MURABBA	Preserves and jams made with spiced fruits or vegetables
MURGH	Chicken
MURGH MAKHANI	Chicken pieces first cooked tandoori-style, then simmered in a butter sauce
MURGH MASSALAM	Whole chicken stuffed and marinated
MURUKKU	Spiced deep-fried spirals made from gram flour, the batter flavoured with ajowan seeds
MUTHU	Pear (South India)

MUZAFFAR	Saffron-flavoured vermicelli with almonds
MYSORE PAK	Fudge-style sweet made from gram flour and nuts

N

NAAN	Tear-drop-shaped leavened bread, cooked in tandoor oven; served plain or with fillings and garnishes
NAAN KHIMA/KHEEMA	Leavened bread (naan) filled with spiced mince and cooked in tandoor oven
NAHARI/NEEHARI	Aromatic dish of lambs' tongues and trotters cooked in a spiced yoghurt sauce often perfumed with sandalwood
NAMAK	Salt
NANDU	Crab (South India)

NARANGI	Orange
NARGISI KOFTA	Hard-boiled egg encased in spiced minced or ground meat, deep-fried and simmered in a mild curry sauce
NARIYAL	Coconut from the palm *Cocos nucifera*
NARIYAL TEL	Coconut oil
NASPATI	General name for pear
NAVRATTAN/NAURATTAN	Meaning nine jewels—a rice dish of nine ingredients named for Moghul emperor Akbar's nine courtiers
NEEM	The Margosa tree (*Azadirachta indica*); the flowers and seeds used for medicinal purposes; the leaves add astringency to food; twigs are used as toothbrushes and the timber serves for firewood
NEERA	Sweet non-intoxicating drink from the sap of the palmyra palm (South India)
NEIPATHAL	Rice-flour dough cut into star shapes and fried (South India)
NIMBU	Lime
NIMBU PANI	Refreshing drink with lime juice

| NIRAMISH | Spiced dish of mixed vegetables |
| NOOSH KHANA | To partake of food or drink |

O

OBLA/UBLA	Boiled
OMPADI	Crunchy savoury nibbles made with gram and rice flour
OOPAMA	Lightly spiced semolina dish (South India)
OOPU	Salt (South India)

P

PAAN	Digestive of chopped areca nut flavoured with camphor, sandalwood and spices, and rolled in a betel leaf
PAALLI/PAPPALI/POPPALI	Papaya, the fruit of the tree *Carica papaya*
PACHADIS	General name for tangy accompaniments made from cooked vegetables or from fruit with yoghurt
PAKORA	Deep-fried vegetable fritters served as a snack

PAKWAN	Deep-fried crisp nibbles made from plain flour and water with a pinch of bicarbonate of soda
PAL	General term for milk (South India)
PALAK	Spinach
PALAPPALAM	Jackfruit, fruit of the tree *Artocarpus integrifolia* (South India)
PALYA	Lightly spiced potato dish (South India)
PANCH PORAN	Five whole spices - mustard, cumin, black onion, fenugreek and fennel seeds mixed in equal proportions—used in vegetable and pulse dishes (Bengal)
PANEER/PANIR	Unfermented soft cheese
PANI	Water
PANI PURI	Puffed up dough discs filled with tamarind juice
PAPETA MA KID	Parsi-style spiced lamb and potatoes
PAPITA	Papaya, the fruit of the tree *Carica papaya*

PAPPAD/PAPPADUM/PAPAR	Lentil wafer
PARANGIKKAL	Pumpkin, *Cucurbita pepo* (South India)
PARATHA/PAROTA	Griddle-fried flaky pastry discs
PARUPU	General name for lentils (South India)
PASANDE	Flattened strips of meat marinated in spices
PATIA	Sweet and sour fish curry (Bombay)
PATISHAPTA	Sweet pancake filled with shredded coconut
PATNA	Long-grain rice
PATRA	Large spinach-like leaf of the taro plant, *Colocasia antiquorum*, spread with a spiced paste, steamed first then fried (Gujarat)
PATRANI MAACHI	Spiced fish cooked in banana leaf (Parsi)
PAU	Unleavened bread rolls served with spiced vegetables as a popular roadside snack (Bombay)
PAU BHAJI	Mixture of spiced vegetables eaten with pau bread

PAYA	Trotters
PAYASA/PAYASAM	Milk pudding dish made from rice; made on festive occasions and as a temple offering
PEG: BURRA, CHOTA	A measure of spirits: burra is a large measure, chota peg, a small
PERA	Fudge-type sweet
PERADA	Soft fudge made from guava
PESARATTO	Lentil pancake with green chillis
PETHA	Ash or wax gourd, *Benincasa hispida*
PHOOL GOBI	Cauliflower
PHULKA	Puffy bread discs
PIAZ/PYAZ	Onion
PILAU/PULAO	Rice dish incorporating meat, chicken or vegetables, with rice in the greater proportion
PIPLI	Long peppers (Capsicum annuum)
PISTA	Pistachio nuts
PODALANGAI	Snake gourd, *Tricosanthus cucumerina* (South India)
PODINA/PUDINA	Mint

POHA	Rice pounded flat
POLIHARAM	Tamarind-flavoured rice (South India)
POMFRET	Fish similar to flounder: either the white pomfret (*Pampus argenteus*) or the black pomfret (*Formio niger*); in Bengal called chanda
PONGAL	Rice dish served in January and February during the South Indian harvest festival of Pongal
POORI/PURI	Wholewheat dough discs that puff up on deep-frying
POOTU/PUTTU	Sweet breakfast dish of pounded rice and coconut (South India)
PORIAL KADAMA	Vegetable dish served during South Indian festival of Pongal
PORIALS	Dry vegetable and coconut dish (South India)
POSTO	Poppy seeds, *Papaver somniferum* (Bengal)
PRASAD/PRASADAM	Foods eaten after first being offered to the gods
PRATHAMAN	Sweet pudding of lentils simmered in coconut milk (South India)

PRESUNTO	Ham marinated in local palm wine (Goa)
PULI	Tamarind, the fleshy pod of the tree *Tamarindus indica* (South India)
PURAN POLI	Flat bread stuffed with sweetened lentils served during the festival of Holi in February/March
PUSHPANNA	Rich rice dish

Q

QABARGAH	Ribbed lamb chops coated with spiced batter (Kashmir)
QABOOLI	Rice and chicken khichdi dish
QUORMA/KORMA	Spiced braised meat, chicken or vegetables

R

RAAN	Spiced, marinated whole leg of lamb
RABRI	Milk reduced to texture of cream by slow simmering without stirring
RAGI	A variety of millet, *Eleusine coracana*, cooked to a brownish mass
RAI	Black mustard seed, *Brassica nigra*
RAITA	Yoghurt-based accompaniment
RAJBHOG	Sweet balls of curd solids immersed in syrup

RAJMA	Whole and unhulled red-brown kidney bean
RAS	Vegetable juice or broth (South India)
RASGULLAS/RASOGOLLAS	Cheesy dough balls in syrup
RASAM	Tamarind-flavoured vegetable broth (South India)
RASAVANGI	Soup-like sauce with miniature eggplant or aubergines (South India)
RASAWADA	Lentil dough balls in a tart sauce (South India)
RASEDAR	Vegetables in a thin sauce (South India)
RASMALAI	Cheesy dough balls, flattened, cooked in syrup and steeped in a cream sauce
RAVA/RAVI	Semolina (South India)
REIACHADO	Prawns or fish marinated in a paste of vinegar and spices, then fried (Goa)
RESHMI KABAB	Minced chicken kabab
RISTA	Meat balls (Kashmir)

ROJAN GOSHT/JOSH	Lamb or goat marinated in tomato based sauce (North India)
ROOMALI/RUMALI ROTI	Superfine wholewheat bread thrown in pizza dough fashion
ROTI	Unleavened bread, baked on a griddle
RUH	Essence
RUH GULAB	Rose essence
RUS	Juice

S

SAAG/SAG — Leafy greens such as spinach

SAAKI/SAKKEI — Jackfruit, fruit of the tree *Artocarpus integrifolia* (South India)

SABAT MOONG — Unhulled whole moong beans, *Phaseolus aureus*

SABJI MANDI — Vegetable market

SABJI/SABZI — A generic term for vegetables

SABU/SABUDANA — Sago: the starchy granules made from the stem of the sago palm (*Metroxylon sagu*)

SAFAID	Dish, usually vegetables, cooked in a white sauce
SAFAIDEE	Eggwhite
SAIJNA DANTA	Long, ridged pods of the tree *Moringa oleifera*, also known as drumstick (Anglo-Indian) because of their shape
SAINDHI	Intoxicating drink, palm liquor
SAMBALS	Accompaniments to curries
SAMBHAR	A sauce usually based on a lentil and vegetable purée (South India)
SAMBHARO	Sweet and sour salad accompaniment (Gujarat)
SAMOOSA	Pastries filled with spiced meat or vegetable then deep-fried
SANDESH/SONDESH	Fudge-like sweet made from fresh cheese curds (Bengal)
SANTARA	Orange (Gujarat)
SARKI	Lentil soup with chopped cucumber and spring onions, served cold
SARSON	Mustard leaves
SASHA	Cucumber (Bengal)

SAUNF/SONF	Fennel seed
SEB	Apple
SEEKH KABAB	Sausage-shaped spiced mince meat, grilled over coals
SEER	The scombroid (mackerel-like) fish *Cybium guttatum*
SEM/SAME	Thin green beans
SENAI/SURAN	Yam, tuber of the genus *Dioscorea* (South India)
SEV	Savoury nibbles made from chick pea-flour batter
SEVIAN	Vermicelli noodles
SHABDEGH	Turnips with kidneys (Lucknow)
SHAHED	Honey
SHAHI	Prefix used to denote dishes that emanate from royal kitchens
SHAHI JEERA	Black cumin seed
SHAHI TUKRE	Exotic bread pudding (Hyderabad)
SHAKARKAND	Sweet potato
SHAKAR	Brown sugar
SHALARI	Celery

SHALGAM	Turnips
SHAMI KABABS	Minced or ground meat first lightly spiced and cooked with lentils then formed into kababs and shallow-fried
SHARBAT/SHERBET	Drinks made from fresh fruit
SHARIFA	Custard apple, the fruit of the tree *Anona squamosa*
SHEERO	Semolina dessert (Gujarat)
SHERMAL/SHIRMAL	Unleavened dough rich with ghee and milk; rolled into discs, brushed with saffron-flavoured milk and baked in the oven
SHORBA	Soup
SHRIKAND	Saffron-flavoured dessert made from yoghurt (Maharashtra)
SHUKTO	Tangy vegetable soup
SIMLA ALU	Tapioca
SIMLA MIRCH	Green bell pepper
SINGARA	Vegetable stuffed pastry shells deep-fried (Bengal)
SIRIPAI	Braised goat's head and feet

SIRKA	Vinegar
SITA PHOOL/SEETHA PHAL	Custard apple, the fruit of the tree *Anona squamosa* (West India)
SOOJI/SUJI	Semolina or farina
SORPOTEL	Pork and liver curry (Goa)
SUAR KA GOSHT/MAAS	Pork
SUNDAL	Chick pea dish (South India)
SUPARI	Finely chopped areca nuts flavoured with camphor and sandalwood, mixed with seeds of cardamom, cumin and fennel, eaten as a digestive on its own or with betel leaf (paan)

T

TABAKMAAS	Spiced lamb rib chops (Kashmir)
TAMARIND	Pulpy sweet and sour flavouring ingredient from the pod of the tree *Tamarindus indica*
TANDOOR	Charcoal-fired clay oven
TANDOORI	Generic name of marinated ingredients cooked in the tandoor oven
TARBOOG/TARBOOZ	Watermelon, *Citrullus lunatus*
TARI	Fermented palm drink

TARKA	Tempering of whole spices or seasonings in hot oil or ghee, added to prepared dishes (South India)
TEESRYO/THISRA	Spiced mussels (Goa)
TEETUR	Partridge or game
TEJ PATTIA/PATTA	Indian bay leaf, from the tree *Cinnamomum cassia*
TEL	Vegetable oil
THAKALI	Tomato (South India)
THALI	Metal circular platter with raised rim; also a complete meal comprising several dishes placed individually in small bowls (katoris) which are placed on the thali in a particular order
THANDAI	Almond milk drink
THANI/THUNNY	Water (South India)
THAYIR	Curds (South India)
THEN	Honey (South India)
THENGAI	Coconut (South India)
THEPLA	Spiced flat bread of wholemeal wheat and gram flour (Gujarat)

TIFFIN	Light meal taken at midday
TIKKA	Pieces of meat, chicken or fish marinated and cooked in tandoor-style clay oven
TIL/TIL KA TEL	Oil extracted from sesame or gingelly seeds, from the plant *Sesamum indicum*
TILAURI	Deep-fried sesame-flavoured gram-flour balls
TINDA	White gourd, *Citrullus vulgaris* var. *fistulosus*
TODDY	Fermented drink from the palmyra or coconut palm
TOOR/TOOVAR DAL	Hulled and split yellow pulse, also known as arhar dal
TOOTAK	Semolina cases filled with spiced mince
TUKMERIA/TOOKMURIA	Small seeds from a plant of the basil family (*Ocimum pilosum*) which swell and form a coating when added to drinks; used to give texture to sherbets
TULSI	Basil plant (*Ocimum basilicum*), considered sacred

U

UBALANA	Boiling
UDIPI	A region of South India noted for its vegetarian food prepared by temple-trained cooks
ULLIPUNDU	Garlic (South India)
ULUNDU VADAI	Lentil patty in a sauce of spiced vegetables (South India)
UPPMA/UPPUMA	Savoury breakfast dish made from semolina or cream of wheat, or vermicelli (South India)

URAD DAL	The unhulled, small black cylindrical pulse is known as sabat urad; when split it becomes chilke urad dal, or simply urad dal when hulled as well as split. The hulled pulse is off-white, not black.
USALI	Pilau-type dish made from lentils
USLI	Ghee (clarified butter)

V

VADDA/VADDAI/WADA	Deep-fried snack of spiced lentils
VANGHIBATH	A dish made with aubergine or eggplant and rice (South India)
VARAK	Edible, tissue-thin sheets of gold or silver used as decoration or garnish
VENGAYAM	Onion (South India)
VENNAY	Butter (South India)
VILAYAITI LASSON	Leeks
VINDALOO	Goan pork dish pungent with chilli
VINHO	Goan grape wine, usually home brewed

WXYZ

WAAZWAAN	Professionally cooked banquet consisting of several lamb dishes (Kashmir)
XACUTTI/XACOOTI	Dish of lamb, chicken or vegetables in a spiced coconut sauce (Goa)
YAKHNI	Rich aromatic meat stock
YERA	Prawns or shrimp (South India)
ZAFFRAN	Dried saffron: whole stigmas or powder from the flowers of the plant *Crocus sativus*
ZAFFRANI PILAU	Saffron-flavoured rice
ZARDA	Sweet rice dish
ZARDALU	Apricot, also known as khoobani
ZARDEE	Egg yolk
ZEERA PANI	Refreshing drink flavoured with cumin and tamarind
ZEERA/ZIRA	Cumin seed

Notes and Additions

INDEX OF CONDIMENTS, FLAVOURINGS, NUTS AND SPICES

Cumin, see FARFAS, JEEB, PANCH PORAN, SUPARI, ZEERA PANI, ZEERA
Curry leaves, see KARHI PATTA, KARIVEPPILAI
Fennel, see PANCH PORAN, SAUNF, SUPARI
Fenugreek, see ALOO METHI, KASOORI, METHI, PANCH PORAN
Garlic, see LASUN, ULLIPUNDU
Ginger, see ADRAK, INGI, KHAGINA
Groundnut, see Peanuts
Jaggery/palm sugar, see AMTI, ATHIRASA, GUR, JAGGERY
Long pepper, see PIPLI
Mace, see JAVATRI
Mango powder, see AAM CHUR
Margosa leaves, see NEEM
Masala, see GARAM MASALA, LAZEEZ
Melon seeds, see CHORMAGAZ
Mint, see PODINA
Mustard seeds/leaves, see KHANDVI, PANCH PORAN, SARSON
Nigella seed, see KALONJI
Nutmeg, see HARISO, JAIPHAL
Nuts, see DOODH PEDA, HALWA, LADDU, MYSORE PAK, see also
        specific varieties
Parsley, see AMJOOD
Peanuts, see KALAKAI, MOONFALLI
Pickle/pickled, see ACHAR
Pine nuts, see CHILGOSE
Pistachio, see PISTA
Poppy seeds, see BHAGHARE BAINGAN, KHUS KHUS, POSTO
Psyllium, see ISABGOL
Safflower seeds, see KARADI
Saffron, see BHAPA DHAI, KESAR, MUZAFFAR, SHERMAL, SHRIKAND,
        ZAFFRAN, ZAFFRANI PILAU
Salt, see NAMAK, OOPU

Sandalwood, see CHANDAN, NAHARI, PAAN, SUPARI

Sesame/gingelly, see BHAGHARE BAINGAN, GINGELLY, KHANDVI, TIL, TILAURI

Spices, see BHAGAR, DHUNAUR, GARAM MASALA, MASALA, TARKA

Star anise, see BADAIN

Sugar, see CHEENEE, CHUKARAI, GANNA, SHAKAR

Tamarind, see AMTI, BHAGHARE BAINGAN, BHEL POORIE, DALCHA, IMLI, KUT, PANI PURI, POLIHARAM, PULI, RASAM, TAMARIND, ZEERA PANI

Turmeric, see HALDI, HALDI PEESI, MANJAL

Vinegar, see SIRKA

Walnut, see AKHROOT

INDEX OF VEGETABLES

Okra, see BHINDI

Onions, see BOORANI, CACHUMBER, DOPIAZA, PIAZ, VENGAYAM

Peas, see ALOO MATTAR, HARE GOBI, KIRIMA, MATTAR

Potatoes, see ALOO, ASSAD, BATATA, BONDA, DUM ALOO, LATCHE,
        PALYA, PAPETA MA KID

Pumpkin, see PARANGIKKAL

Radish, see BAFFAD, MOOLE

Snake gourd, see CHICHINGA, PODALANGAI

Spinach, see ALOO PALAK, CALDO VERDE, PALAK, SAAG

Spring onion, see SARKI

Sweet potato, see SHAKARKAND

Tapioca, see SIMLA ALU

Taro, see Colocasia

Tomatoes, see CACHUMBER, KUT, ROJAN GOSHT, THAKALI

Turnips, see SHABDEGH, SHALGAM

Vegetables, general, see AVIYAL, BHARTA, BHUKI, CALDINE,
        CHARCHARI, FOOGATH, GOJJU, HALWA, KOFTAS, KOORAL,
        KOOTUS, KORMA, LAPHRA, MURABBA, NIRAMISH,
        PACHADIS, PAU BHAJI, PORIAL KADAMA, PORIALS, QUORMA,
        RASEDAR, SABJI, SAFAID, SAMOOSA, SINGARA, TIKKA,
        ULUNDU VADAI, XACUTTI

Wax gourd, see Ash gourd

White gourd, see TILAURI

Yam, see JAMIKAND, SENAI

INDEX OF FRUIT

Raisins/sultanas, see KISH MISH
Starfruit, see KAMARAKH
Sugarcane, see GANNA
Sultanas, see MUNACCA
Watermelon, see TARBOOG
Woodapple, see KAITH

INDEX OF BREAD, CEREALS, LEGUMES AND PULSES

Rice, see ARISI, ARWA CHAVAL, BAKALA BATH, BALAM, BASMATI, BEVECA, BHAT, BIRYANI, CHAWAL, CHENNEL, DHAN, DOODH PAK, DUM PHUKT, KANJI, KHICHDI, LAZIZAN, NAVRATTAN, PATNA, PAYASA, PILAU, POLIHARAM, PONGAL, PUSHPANNA, QABOOLI, VANGHIBATH, ZAFFRANI PILAU, ZARDA

Rice, flattened, see AVIL UPPUMA, POHA, POOTU

Rice flour, see Flour, rice

Rice, puffed, see MOORI

Sago, see SABU

Semolina/cream of wheat, see CURAMBA, KESARI, LADDU, OOPAMA, RAVA, SHEERO, SOOJI, TOOTAK, UPPMA

Vermicelli, see KESARI, MUZAFFAR, SEVIAN, UPPMA

Wheat, cracked, see DALIA, GAIHUN, HALEEM, HARISSA, KHAMIR

Wheat, see also Flour, wheat

INDEX OF MEAT

INDEX OF GAME AND POULTRY

INDEX OF FISH AND SEAFOOD

INDEX OF SNACKS, SOUPS AND SWEETS

INDEX OF DAIRY PRODUCTS

INDEX OF MISCELLANEOUS ITEMS

BIBLIOGRAPHY

Achaya, K.T., *Indian Food, An Historical Companion*, OUP, Delhi, 1994

Attwood, Mary, *A Taste of India*, Houghton Mifflin Company, Boston, 1969

Aziz, Khalid, *Step by Step Guide to Indian Cooking*, Hamlyn, New York 1974

Ballentine, Martha, *Himalayan Mountain Cookery; A Vegetarian Cookbook*, Himalayan International Institute, Pennsylvania 1986

Chapman, Pat, *250 Favourite Curries and Accompaniments*, Judy Piatkus, London 1992

Collins, Ruth Philpott, *A World of Curries*, Avenel Books, New York 1958

Dandekar, Hermalata C., Illustrations by Johnson, B.L., *Beyond Curry*, Centre for South and Southeast Asian Studies, The University of Michigan, USA 1984

Dandekar, Varsha, *Salads of India*, The Crossing Press, New York, 1983

Dasa, Adiraja, *The Hare Krishna Book of Vegetarian Cooking*, The Bhaktivedanta Book Trust, Los Angeles 1984

Davidson, Alan, *Seafood of South-East Asia*, Federal Publications, Singapore, 1977

Devi, Yamuna, *The Best of Lord Krishna's Cuisine*, Bala Books, California 1991

Devi, Yamuna, *Yamuna's Table*, Button Books, Penguin, USA 1992

Gupta, Pranati Sen, *The Art of Indian Cuisine*, Hawthorn Books Inc., New York 1974

The Hare Krishna Cookbook compiled by Drsna Devi Dasi and Sama Devi Dasi, The Bhaktivedanta Book Trust, Los Angeles, 1973

The Higher Taste, The Bhaktivedanta Book Trust, Los Angeles, 1984

Jaffrey, Madhur, *A Taste of India*, Pavilion, London, 1985

Jain, Laymi and Manoj, *Melody of Indian Cuisine*, Woodbridge Press, California 1992

Kaur, Bibiji Inderjit, *A Taste of India*, Areline Publications, Pomona/Berkeley, 1985

Kirchner, Bharti, *Indian Inspired; A New Cuisine for the International Table*, Lovell House, Los Angeles, 1993

Madavan, Vijay, *Cooking the Indian Way*, Lerner Publication Company, Minneapolis, 1985

Mehta, Shahnaz with Korenblit, Joan, *Good Cooking from India*, Roidale Press, Emmaus, Pennsylvania, 1981

Moore, Isabel, *Indian Cooking*, Marshall Cavendish, London/New York 1977

Pandya, Michael, *Complete Indian Cookbook*, Hamlyn, London/New York, 1980

Passmore, Jackie, *Asian Cookery in Colour*, Paul Hamlyn Pty Ltd., New York, 1979

Philip, Thangam E., *Modern Cookery for Teaching and the Trade*, Vol. I, Orient Longman, New Delhi, 1988

Rad, Shivaji and Holkab, Shalini Devi, *Cooking of the Maharajas*, The Viking Press, New York, 1975

Rani, *Feast of India*, Contemporary Books, Chicago, 1991

Rosengarten, Frederic, *The Book of Spices*, Pyramid Books, New York, 1973

Sacharoff, Shanta Nimbark, *Flavours of India*, 101 Productions, California, 1976

Sahni, Julie, *Classic Indian Cooking*, William Morrow and Company Inc., New York, 1980

Shirley, Jo Ann, *Wonderful Ways to prepare Curries*, Playmore Inc., New York, 1978

Singh, Dharman Jit, *Classical Cooking from India*, Houghton Mifflin Company, Boston, 1956

Singh, Manja Shirvat, *The Spice Box, Vegetarian Indian Cookbook*, The Crossing Press, New York, 1981

Solomon, Charmaine, *The Complete Asian Cookbook*, Weldon, Sydney, 1992

Stobart, Tom, *The Cook's Encyclopaedia*, Papermac, London, 1982

Tiruchelvam, Sharmini, *Food of the Orient; India*, Marshall Cavendish, New York, 1978

Vanamali, *The Taste Divine Indian Vegetarian Cooking the Natural Way*, State University of New York Press, 1993

NOTES AND ADDITIONS

NOTES AND ADDITIONS

Notes and Additions